CHADDERTON

MICHAEL LAWSON & MARK JOHNSON

Published by
Oldham Leisure Services
© Oldham Leisure Services 1990
Civic Centre, West St, Oldham

ISBN 0 902809 23 7

Designed by Oldham Leisure Services.
Printed by Snape Printers Ltd.
Oldham Road, Manchester M35 0AA

The authors wish to thank fellow members of the Chadderton Historical Society for the support and enthusiasm given to this project and to the following for photographs and information:

Lady Maureen Black (Radclyffe of Foxdenton); National Portrait Gallery, London; Sothebys, London; Shire Hall, Lancaster; Lancashire County Record Office, Preston; Local Studies Library, Oldham; Chadderton Library; Middleton Library; Evening Chronicle, Oldham; St. Matthew's Parochial Church Council; St. Luke's Parochial Church Council; Christ Church Parochial Church Council; Trustees of Healds Green Institute; Mrs. E. Elly for the Harold Elly Collection; Mr. H. Holmes of British Aerospace; Mr. L. Boon; Mr. W. Helliwell; Mr. D. H. Smith; Mr. J. Briggs; Mr. R. J. Magee; Mr. E. Edge; Mrs. D. Smith; Mr. A. Lees; Mrs. E. Green; Mr. H. Pleasant; Mrs. F. Arnold; Mrs. I. Scarsbrook; Mrs. F. Green; Mr. M. Warrington; Mr. T. Smith; Mr. B. M. Edge; Mrs. P. Struthers; Mrs. M. Eastwood; Mrs. G. Fitton; Mr. A. Brierley; Mr. C. S. MacDonald; Mr. M. Greenwood; Mr. W. Billington; Mrs. P. Hyde and Mr. A. Kirby and Mr. R. Dunning of Manchester Transport Museum Society. Attempts have been made to trace the owners of all photographs and the authors wish to apologise for any omissions which may have occurred.

Thanks are also due to Mr. Richard Lambert and Mrs. Terry Berry, Oldham Leisure Services, for their help and advice during the preparation stage.

The authors:
Michael Lawson is a local headteacher and Secretary
of the Chadderton Historical Society. He is the author of "Chadderton Chapters".
Mark Johnson, a sales manager, is Chairman of the Society.

*This pictorial history is dedicated to the memory of Herbert Buckley,
Fred Dale, William Johnson, Frank Orson, Vera Schofield and Vincent Taylor,
deceased members of the Chadderton Historical Society.*

An inglenook in Chadderton Fold. This painting by J. Houghton Hague captures the atmosphere of the old community as it existed in the 19th century.

Before the re-organisation of local government in 1974, Chadderton was a local authority situated in the south-east of the historic county of Lancashire. At that date it joined with six neighbouring authorities to form the Metropolitan Borough of Oldham which in turn became one of the ten districts of the newly-created County of Greater Manchester.

The name Streetbridge suggests that the Romans marched through the area, whilst the name, derived from Cadertun – the settlement of the hill-fort – indicates Celtic and Anglo-Saxon influences. A tumulus or ancient burial mound also dated from this period and is marked on maps even at the end of the nineteenth century.

During the Middle Ages several grants of land in Chadderton were made to various religious orders. The canons of Cockersand Abbey, near Lancaster, held land near Foxdenton whilst those at Stanlaw Abbey in Cheshire had land whose boundaries included Tachelache (Thatch Leach) and Caule Shaw (Coalshaw Green). The crusading order of Knights Hospitallers, who were founded to help Christian pilgrims to the Holy Land, also held land locally.

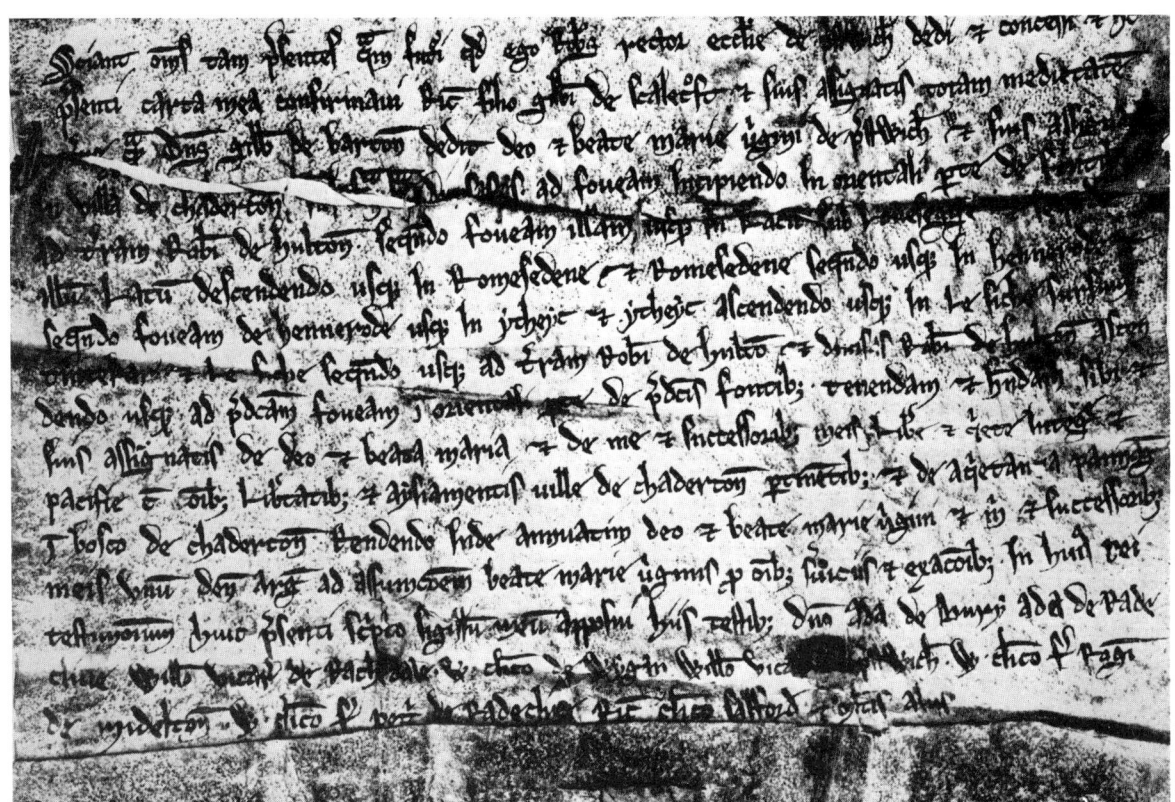

Know all men . . . that I, Robert, Rector of Prestwich . . . have given . . . to Richard son of Gilbert of Scalecroft . . . land . . . in the township of Chaderton . . . rendering yearly . . . to me and my successors one silver penny at the Assumption of the Blessed Virgin Mary . . .

This document from around 1220, is the earliest still in existence which relates to Chadderton. Among the witnesses to this grant of land in the Mills Hill area are William of Radcliffe, Adam of Bury, William, vicar of Rochdale, William, son of Roger of Middleton, and Richard, clerk of Salford.

For religious purposes Chadderton lay within the extensive parish of Prestwich-cum-Oldham with its neighbours Royton, Oldham and Crompton. The manorial government, however, was quite different.

Unlike these three townships Chadderton had the distinction of being a constituent manor of the Estate or Fee of Tottington whose great overlords by the thirteenth century were the De Lacys, Barons of Clitheroe Castle.

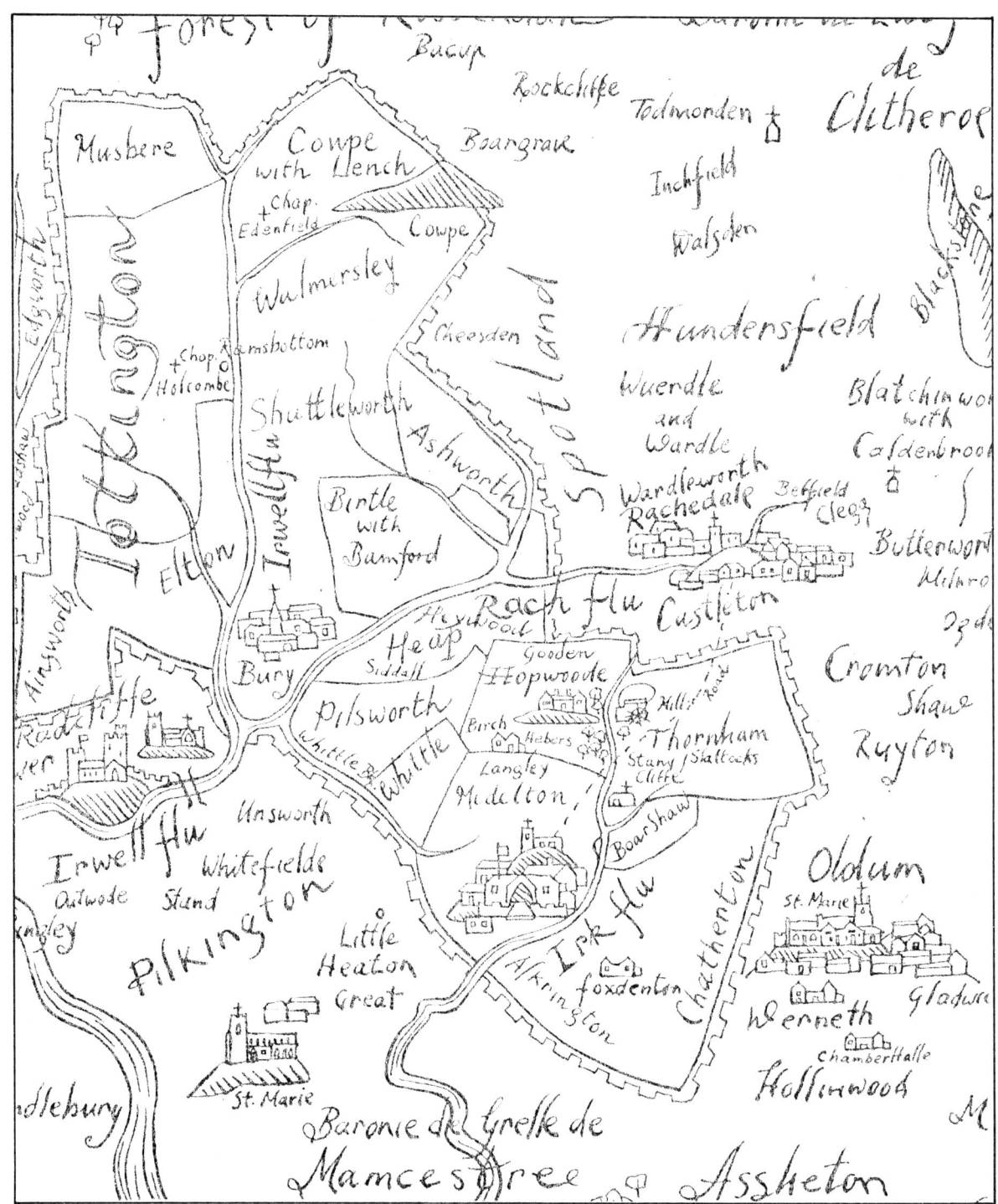

This early map portrays the ancient Fee or Estate of Tottington which included Chadderton within its south-east boundary. The estate dated back to Norman times when its overlord was Baron Montbegon of Hornby Castle near Lancaster. The Montbegons were a powerful family with vast estates in the north of England granted by William the Conqueror.

During the thirteenth century Geoffrey de Chadderton became the Lord of the Manor. His descendants were to make their mark nationally in later centuries. William Chadderton became Bishop of Chester (the diocese then covering our area), whilst Laurence Chadderton, the first Master of Emmanuel College, Cambridge, was one of the co-translators of the King James Bible of 1611.

After the division of the manor in the mid-fifteenth century there came a succession of notable families – Radcliffe, Assheton and Horton, whose importance was not confined to the township. The ancient halls at Chadderton and Foxdenton were to provide six High Sheriffs to Lancashire whilst knighthoods were to be received and friendships with monarchs forged.

The landscape at this time was a rural one with farms scattered on gently undulating ground among the many streams which crossed the township. The centre of the township was in Chadderton Fold where the manor house, manorial corn mill and a few cottages lay alongside the River Irk. There was, however, no parish church overlooking the Fold until the mid-nineteenth century.

Above: Hunt Lane Farm, dating from before the 19th century, was demolished around 1914 when the railway line to the Chadderton Goods Yard was constructed. (Drawing by J. Herbert Heywood).

Left: William Chadderton, Bishop of Chester 1579-1595, and then of Lincoln. Known as the 'Good Bishop' he was the great-uncle of Margaret Radclyffe of Foxdenton Hall. In 1582 he married off his nine-year old daughter to an eleven-year-old boy!
(Reproduced by kind permission of the Lord Bishop of Chester and the Church Commissioners for England).

Before the mid-eighteenth century, the population numbered less than one thousand and were occupied on the land and in cottage industries, including fustian and silk weaving. A fulling mill, dating back to Elizabethan times, was in operation on the River Irk below Chadderton Fold. As the agricultural landscape and community vanished before the onslaught of the Industrial Revolution cotton spinning became the dominant source of employment. Nearly sixty mills were to be constructed between 1776, when the water-powered Bank Mill was built on the Stock Brook, and 1926, when the last traditional mill in the county, the Elk, was constructed beside the newly-opened Broadway.

Early cotton mill at Birchen Bower, 1829

Other industries which were dependent on cotton spinning also came into prominence during this period with textile engineering and coal mining much in evidence. Advances in the means of transportation and communication resulted in feats such as the Rochdale Canal (1804) and the Manchester to Leeds Railway (1839), the former gently curving its way around the valley of the River Irk whilst the latter strides over the valley on an impressive embankment. A station at Mills Hill was Chadderton's first link with the railway network.

During the nineteenth century a new administrative centre evolved along the turnpike road between Middleton and Oldham. This was more central and accessible to the growing town than Chadderton Fold. At the same time other hamlets within the township, notably Butler Green, Cowhill and Middleton Junction developed as thriving communities.

Th' Iron Donger, built by Messrs Radford of Manchester in 1838, carried the railway over the canal near Mills Hill. Although now unused it is still in position next to its more modern counterpart.

URBAN SANITARY AUTHORITY FOR DISTRICT OF CHADDERTON	School Attendance Committee
Names & Addresses of Members.	**NAMES OF MEMBERS.**
1 JOHN MURGATROYD, ESQ. *Chairman.* Sunnyside, Hollinwood.	1 RALPH BAGLEY, ESQ., *Chairman.* Mornington House, Middleton Road.
2 MR. WILLIAM TAYLOR, Belton Place.	2 MR. JOHN MURGATROYD, Sunnyside, Hollinwood.
3 ,, JAMES CHADWICK, Wykeham Place.	3 ,, WILLIAM TAYLOR, Belton Place.
4 ,, LEVI LAMBERT, Middleton Road.	4 ,, JAMES CHADWICK, Wykeham Place.
5 ,, JAMES HEGINBOTTOM, Dalton Street.	5 ,, LEVI LAMBERT, Middleton Road.
6 ,, CHRISTOPHER MOORE, Lansdown Rd.	6 ,, CHRISTOPHER MOORE, Lansdown Rd.
7 ,, JOHN ASHWORTH, Longsight, Oldham.	7 ,, JOHN SCHOFIELD, Street Bridge.
8 ,, JOHN SCHOFIELD, Street Bridge.	8 ,, THOMAS H. SMETHURST, Stock Lane
9 ,, THOMAS H. SMETHURST, Stock Lane	9 ,, WILLIAM LEES, Manchester Road, Hollinwood.
10 ,, RALPH BAGLEY, Middleton Road.	10 ,, JOHN HILTON, Dalton Street,
11 ,, WILLIAM LEES, Manchester Road, Hollinwood.	11 ,, MILES CROMPTON, Foxdenton Lane.
12 ,, JOHN HILTON, Dalton Street.	12 ,, JONATHAN PARTINGTON, Grimshaw Lane.
13 ,, MILES CROMPTON, Foxdenton Lane.	**CLERK.** F. TWEEDALE, Chadderton.
14 ,, JONATHAN PARTINGTON, Grimshaw Lane.	**SCHOOL ATTENDANCE OFFICER.** SAMUEL BURGESS, Mills Hill, Chadderton.
15 ,, WILLIAM HASLAM, Birchenlee Street.	
Committees.	**Officers of the Authority.**
SANITARY COMMITTEE. SURVEYOR'S DO. FINANCE & GENERAL PURPOSES DO. *These Committees are each constituted of the whole of the Members of the Board.*	**MEDICAL OFFICER OF HEALTH.** THOMAS PATTERSON, M.D. **CLERK.** F. TWEEDALE. **SURVEYOR.** JOHN SHORE, 399, Middleton Road. **COLLECTOR.** WILLIAM OGDEN, 69, Busk Street. **NUISANCE INSPECTOR.** W. G. ADKINSON, 261, Burnley Lane.

Members of Chadderton Local Board and School Attendance Committee in 1881-82. Belton Place was on the site of the present Town Hall whilst Wykeham Place disappeared when the Baths and Library were built. There were a number of these mid-Victorian mill-owners houses in the centre of Chadderton. A row of three named 'Rushbank' still exists next to the Town Hall.

Chadderton gained representation in Parliament in 1832, when it became part of the Oldham Parliamentary Borough with William Cobbett and John Fielding elected as M.Ps.

In 1873, a Local Board was elected to govern the township and in 1894, this was reconstituted as an Urban District Council of eighteen members. By the 1930's Chadderton was the second largest urban district in Britain's most populous county and in addition to its local powers also elected two representatives to the Lancashire County Council which sat at Preston. Initial steps were also taken during this period to change the status of the town from urban district to municipal borough, which would have given Chadderton its mayor and increased prestige but the matter was eventually put in abeyance.

As the cotton industry went into decline after the First World War, Chadderton was again to make its contribution to the nation, this time through its newer industries. British Aerospace's programme regularly includes projects for Britain's defence whilst government forms, irritating though they may be, are printed at Her Majesty's Stationery Office. Modern technology has been represented for many decades by Ferranti whilst the latest newcomer to Chadderton is the newspaper printing works of Robert Maxwell.

Ralph Bagley, the Chairman of the School Attendance Committee. In 1883-84 he served as Chairman of the Local Board. His residence, Mornington House, still exists as 437 Middleton Road, opposite the Town Hall.

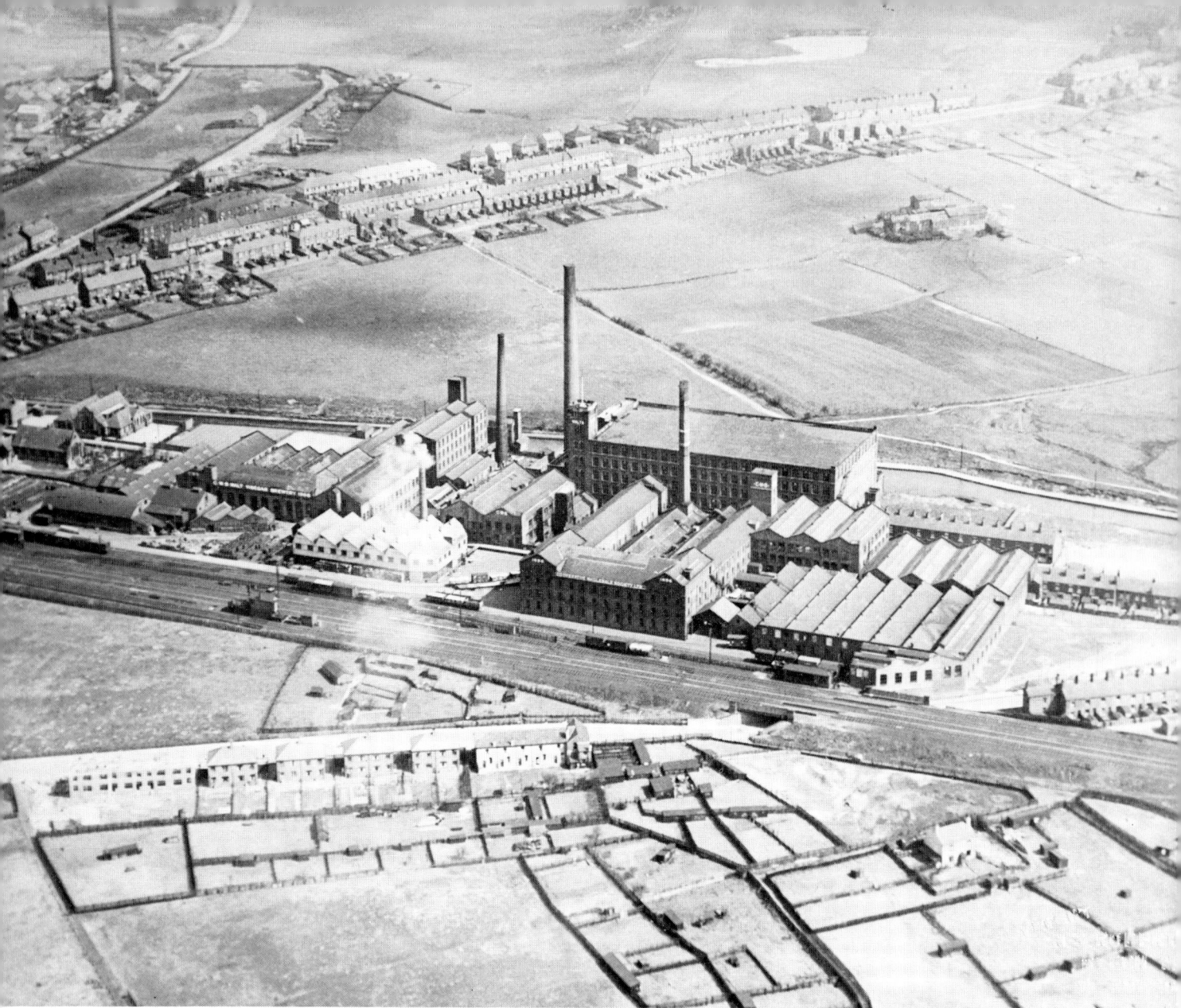

Western Chadderton in the 1930's with Mills Hill Road in the foreground and Middleton Road crossing the picture. McDougall's Chemical Works in the upper left-hand corner has given way to the Irk Vale Estate whilst the Rydal Avenue development now covers the open land above Middleton Road. Roughs Farm seen amid open fields to right of centre has also disappeared beneath the extensive Drummer Hill and Firwood Park Estates.

Population growth has accompanied industrial growth and the inhabitants of Chadderton now number some 33,000. Indeed, a feature of the town in the past quarter of a century has been the development of several housing estates in the rural western half of the district including, at Firwood Park, the largest private estate in Europe. At the same time new shopping, health and leisure facilities have been a part of the town centre re-development.

This pictorial record, containing photographs and other visual material, is an attempt to recall these past centuries not only with a sense of nostalgia and pride but with the desire to preserve and pass on to future generations that part of Chadderton's rich heritage which we still possess.

Michael Lawson, Chadderton 1990.

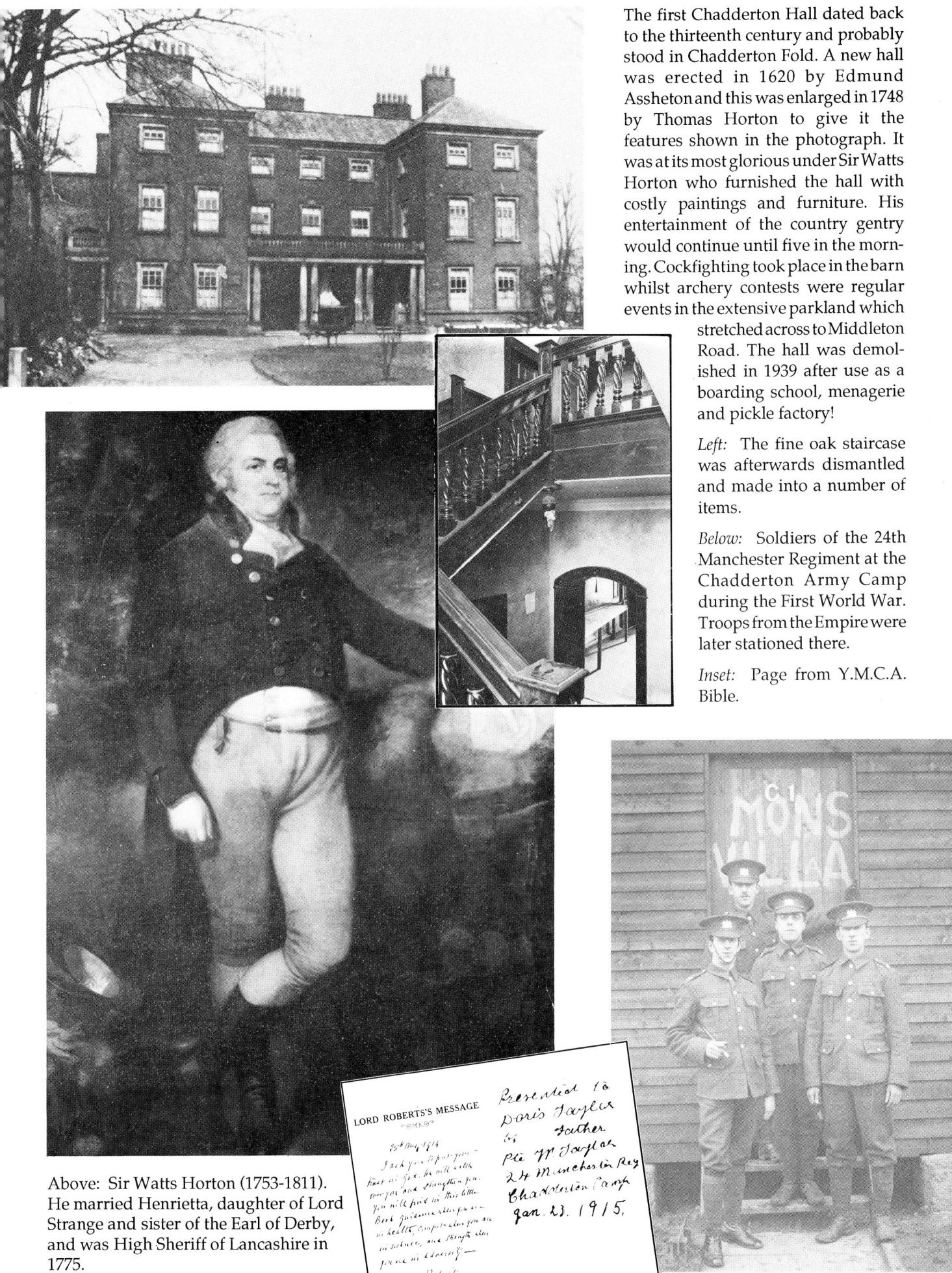

The first Chadderton Hall dated back to the thirteenth century and probably stood in Chadderton Fold. A new hall was erected in 1620 by Edmund Assheton and this was enlarged in 1748 by Thomas Horton to give it the features shown in the photograph. It was at its most glorious under Sir Watts Horton who furnished the hall with costly paintings and furniture. His entertainment of the country gentry would continue until five in the morning. Cockfighting took place in the barn whilst archery contests were regular events in the extensive parkland which stretched across to Middleton Road. The hall was demolished in 1939 after use as a boarding school, menagerie and pickle factory!

Left: The fine oak staircase was afterwards dismantled and made into a number of items.

Below: Soldiers of the 24th Manchester Regiment at the Chadderton Army Camp during the First World War. Troops from the Empire were later stationed there.

Inset: Page from Y.M.C.A. Bible.

Above: Sir Watts Horton (1753-1811). He married Henrietta, daughter of Lord Strange and sister of the Earl of Derby, and was High Sheriff of Lancashire in 1775.
(The present owner of this portrait is not known).

Local lion, Chang, dies (1897)

On Sunday afternoon at a quarter past three, before a number of cotton spinners, mill managers and bank managers, the famous lion "Chang" passed peacefully away at Chadderton Hall, and in its demise, Mr. Jos. Ball has sustained a great loss, inasmuch as the lion was, if not the largest and most handsome of its species in the country, at all events one of them. It was the most recent purchase of its kind at Chadderton Hall. A fortnight ago it got a cold which developed into inflammation of the lungs. "Chang" had medicine put in his milk, but all to no avail. The animal, four years old, had been the admiration of thousands of visitors to Chadderton.

Chadderton Hall in 1905 with the stable block to its right. At the left of the gateposts (which still exist) can be seen the turnstiles through which thousands of visitors passed.

For several years commencing in 1896, Chadderton Hall and grounds became a pleasure garden, a well-known spot for relaxation. A menagerie with crocodiles, bears, monkeys, a boxing kangaroo and "Chang – the largest and grandest lion ever known" was an immediate success until the climate and financial difficulties intervened. Boating lasted longer – until the lake was breached in the great storm of 1927.

Below: May Livsey, whose family manufacturered pickles and preserves at the Hall, proudly sits astride a horse belonging to the Army Camp.

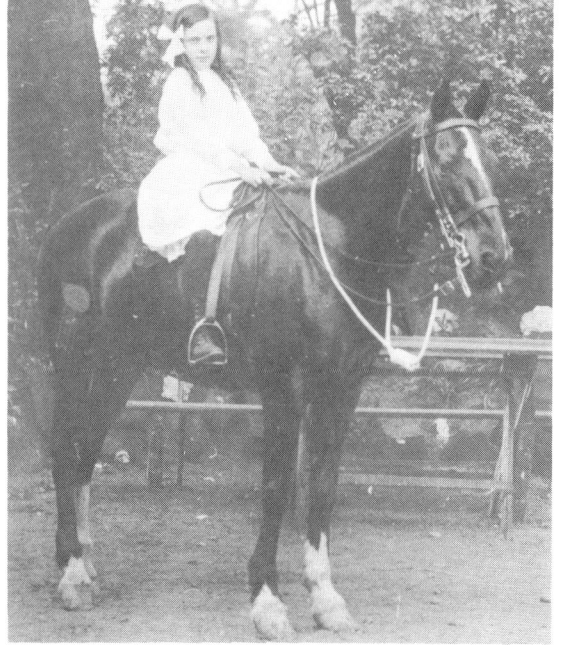

Bishop Lake's House, Chadderton Fold, about 1880. John Lake lived there from 1650 to 1654 when he was minister at the parish church in Oldham. He was forced to resign during the Presbyterian controversy which threatened the Church of England. He later became Bishop of Sodor and Man, then of Bristol and finally of Chichester. It was in this last See that he became known to history as one of the seven bishops who refused to read King James II's declaration of conscience, believing that the king favoured Roman Catholicism to the detriment of the established church.

This nineteenth century group is seen outside the Cow and Calf public house, which occupied part of Bishop Lake's house. This historic house was demolished in 1962.

The first Foxdenton Hall, of which we have no record, was erected in the mid-fifteenth century when the manor was divided and a home was needed for the Radclyffes who became joint lords with the Asshetons of Chadderton Hall. A second hall was built in 1620 and the ground floor of that building now forms the basement of the present hall which dates from 1700. The photograph shows the south front about the turn of this century.

Foxdenton Hall Farm about the beginning of the century. With its great barn (not shown) it was the home farm of the Radclyffes.

Sir Richard Radcliffe of Newcroft, Urmston. He came into possession of the Manor in 1579 by his marriage to his relative, Margaret Radcliffe of Foxdenton. Her great-uncle was the "Good Bishop" William Chadderton of Chester.

Colonel Sir William Radcliffe – the "Foxdenton Redhead", who inherited the Manor in 1642. A loyal supporter of Charles I he was knighted at the Battle of Lostwithiel in 1644. He died in Chadderton three years later.

Alexander Radclyffe, 1677-1735, who built the present hall. His grandson, Robert, 1737-1783, was the last Radclyffe to be born there before the family bought other properties in Dorset.

Foxdenton Park and Hall were leased to Chadderton Council by the Radclyffe family in 1922, and opened to the public. By 1960, when the council became owners of the property, the hall was in a very dangerous condition. After much controversy the decision was made to restore the hall to its original state and the work, which took almost two years, was completed in 1965.

Both these photographs were taken in the 1920's. The bowling green is still as popular but the putting green shown in the lower picture has been replaced by tennis courts.

In June 1937 the last Radclyffe of Foxdenton, Major Charles Robert Eustace, visited the town to open the new bowling green at North Chadderton Social Club, Broadway. He is pictured between his wife and the Chairman of the Council, Thomas Hilton. On the far left is Councillor Brabin with the Clerk to the Council, Mr. J. Schofield.

Above: Chadderton Fold early this century. This was the ancient centre of the township and escaped industrialisation. The house at the left was known as Bishop Lake's and possibly incorporated the medieval Chadderton Hall.

"Tick a' window" at Streetbridge on the boundary with Royton. Demolished since this photograph was taken in 1965, this shop served its customers through the small window in the side of the building.

Previously it had a long history as a public house – known finally as the "Old Engine". A directory of 1818 describes the inn with the couplet:

"Altho' the Engine's smoke be black!
If you'll walk in I've ale like sack".

The inset photo was taken about 1920 shortly before it closed.

An early photograph of the group of cottages at Top of Cragg. The building to the right was Logwood Mill which incorporated the ancient manorial corn mill. The corn mill was powered by the River Irk and during the Middle Ages all the inhabitants of Chadderton were obliged to use it for grinding their corn.

The Rose of Lancaster, Haigh Lane, before modernisation. Note the horse trough in the courtyard. The inn stands on the ancient road from Middleton to Chadderton Hall and on to Oldham and was the meeting place early last century for local Jacobites and other radicals. It was no doubt frequented by James Jackson of nearby Acres Farm who served seven years transportation to Australia for his political activities.

Nordens Branch of the Co-op a few years after its opening in 1910. The wooden hut was the temporary building and was known as a "Klondike" co-op. Fish World and Video World now occupy the premises.

Taken at the the end of the nineteenth century this photograph shows members of the Thompson Family of Burnley Lane Farm. The houses are 374 to 378 Burnley Lane adjacent to the Rifle Range Inn.

Chadderton Hall Road in the early years of this century. St. Matthew's Church is seen in the rural surroundings which have largely survived to the present time.

Below: Chadderton Park Road in the early 1920's seen as little more than an unmetalled track from its Middleton Road end. The parkland it crosses was the venue in the late 18th century for archery contests organised by Sir Watts Horton. Early last century cavalry reviews in the park attracted large crowds of spectators.

Woodside Farm, demolished in the early 1970's when the motorway was cut through Chadderton Heights.

Right: Burnley Lane Farm, seen here about 1920, was another victim of the motorway. It stood where the Broadway roundabout now is.

Below: Possibly the oldest building in Chadderton, Foxdenton Farmhouse with its cruck frame (inset) could date back to mediaeval times. It may have been the first manor house of the Radclyffe family before the later halls were built.

Taken about 1890, this photograph shows Stock Brook School (1859-1986) with the Palm Mill in the background. The mill, erected in 1884, had an extra storey added in 1899 and was demolished in 1926.

FRED BROOK,
Coal ✦ Merchant,
25, Queens Road, Chadderton.

Orders for Loads or Bags of Coal promptly attended to.

J. B. WOODHOUSE,
TEACHER OF
Pianoforte, Organ,
AND
Theory of Music.

TERMS: APPLY
69, Queen's Road, Chadderton.

Stockbrook Sick and Burial Society.

The Committee desire to draw the attention of the public to the following Scale of Payments and Benefits:—

Class Age Children 1 to 10 years	Entrance Fee	Cons. per month.	Sick Benefits				Funeral £ s. d.
			1st 10 weeks	2nd 10 weeks	3rd 10 weeks	4th 20 weeks	3 mts. 1 10 0 6 mts. 3 0 0 12 mts. 4 10 0 £ s. d.
1.— 6 to 30	2d.	2d.	2/-	1/6	1/-	8d.	2 0 0
2.—10 to 30	3d.	5d.	4/-	2/-	1/6	1/-	4 0 0
3.—15 to 30	4d.	7½d.	6/-	3/-	2/-	1/6	6 0 0
4.—(Males) 18 to 30	6d.	10d.	8/-	4/6	3/-	2/-	8 0 0

Further information will be given on application to the Secretary, Robert Sutcliffe, 43, Queen's Road, Chadderton.

Queens Road about 1920. The former vicarage of St. Luke's church can be seen in the centre of the photograph whilst the gates across the road marked the grounds of the Hamilton family who were local benefactors. The advertisements come from the first decade of this century.

Two views of Washbrook in the late nineteenth century. Butler Green Post Office was then situated near the corner of Washbrook and Stanley Road. Later it was moved across the road to Butler Green before moving to its present premises about 1970.

"Finest Lancashire Cheese", "Real Irish Butter". The day of the corner shop is recalled by this 1930's view of Duckworth's shop at Butler Green.

Chadderton Church

Until the middle of the nineteenth century there was no parish church in Chadderton. In 1844, under the New Parishes Act, the parish of St. Matthew was formed and services held in the stables of Chadderton Hall.

Rev. J. R. Dunne, first vicar (1844-69).

The temporary wooden church opened in 1848 at Cragg on the banks of the River Irk.

The northern end of Chadderton Park Road as it looked early this century. The imposing St. Matthew's vicarage on Nordens Road, built in 1878, was demolished shortly after it became redundant in 1956. Chadderton Hall may be picked out among the trees to the left whilst the large barn of Chadderton Hall Farm occupies the centre of the photograph. The field to the left was the site of the army camp during the Great War.

A Tale of Two Steeples! *(Above):* The upper photograph shows Chadderton Church before the steeple was added in 1881. The church was opened in 1857 by the first Bishop of Manchester, Dr. J. Prince-Lee.

Left: The architect's impression of 1882 shows St. Luke's Church with a magnificent tower and spire reaching to a height of 57 metres. Unfortunately these were never built. However, with a height of 21 metres the church is still an imposing structure and in the days of the urban district council was used for civic services.

A rally of the Chadderton Band of Hope about 1920 on ground off Garforth Street where the Congregational Church now stands. The mill is the Hawthorn which, when demolished in 1971, was Lancashire's last all-mule spinning mill. The dome of the Manor Mill appears above the centre of the picture.

PUBLIC ✤ CLOCK.

To the Inhabitants of Washbrook, Butler Green and Neighbourhood.

Dear Friends,

We have pleasure in stating that the Clock erected in the Tower of the Primitive Methodist New Chapel, Washbrook, and subscribed for by public subscription, WILL BE STARTED on Saturday Afternoon, March 11th, 1893, by CLEMENT J. HALL, Esq., Chamber Cottage, Hollinwood.

A PROCESSION

Will form at the School at 3 o'clock, headed by the Park Estate Brass Band, and proceed through the village, &c. All the Inhabitants are urged to join in this procession.

After the starting of the Clock, a short Service will be held in the Chapel, to be conducted by the Rev. J. PRESTWICH, (Resident Minister,) and an Address given by the Rev. DANZY SHEEN, of Middleton. A TEA will be provided at the close, followed by a PUBLIC MEETING. Tickets 6d. each.

Hoping you will all come and join in this great undertaking,

Yours truly,

THE COMMITTEE.

Once a familiar landmark at the Butler Green crossroads was the clocktower of Washbrook Methodist Church which opened in 1893. The original church and schoolroom can be seen to the left and dated from 1868. An institute was also added in 1912 but the whole complex was demolished about 1970.

Butler Green as it appeared in the 1930's. The Whit procession is returning to the Washbrook Methodist Church at the right of the picture. This area was totally redeveloped in the early 1970's and only the Stanley Road railway bridge and the terrace row to the right of it remain.

A daughter church of Christ Church, this temporary building stood on Denton Lane until the new St. Saviour's was built in the 1960's. Because of structural faults this church was abandoned and a third church erected near the new Christ Church Primary School.

Top left: The "Tin Church" which served St. Herbert's Catholic Parish from 1917 until the present church was erected in 1957. When it was built it was on Park Street which was later incorporated into Broadway.

Top right: The Working Men's Mission at Old Lane was opened in 1894. An extension was later added to this building.

Left: Cowhill Methodist Church and Sunday School opened in 1855 on Block Lane. It was demolished about 1970 when local Methodists moved to their new South Chadderton Church on Thompson Lane.

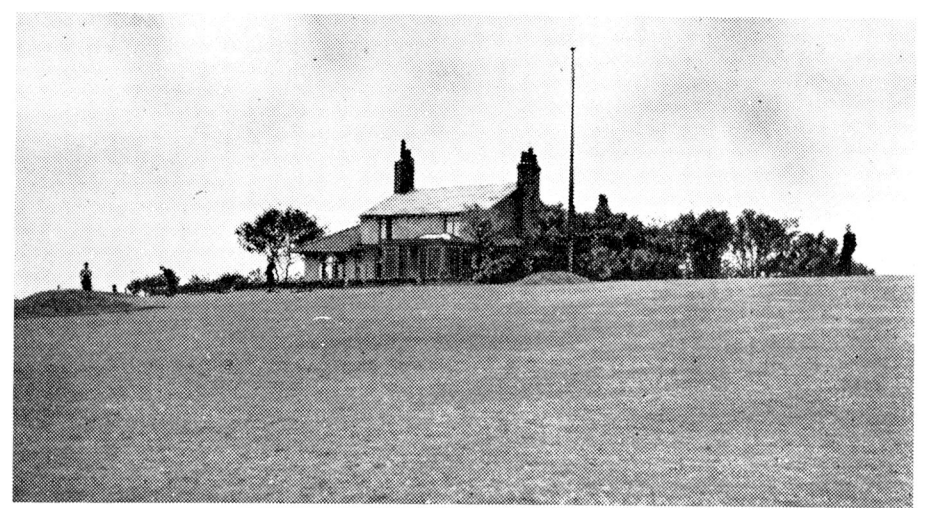

The club house and eighteenth green at Chadderton Golf Club in the 1930's. The club was based at Acres above Chadderton Fold and closed down in 1941.

Below right: Dating from the first decade of this century this atlas was used in local schools. It contained a map of Chadderton as well as the usual world-wide maps.

Below left: Healds Green Methodist Church on an "Old Sing" day in 1927. This church was erected in 1865 and became the Sunday School on the construction of the present church in 1929.

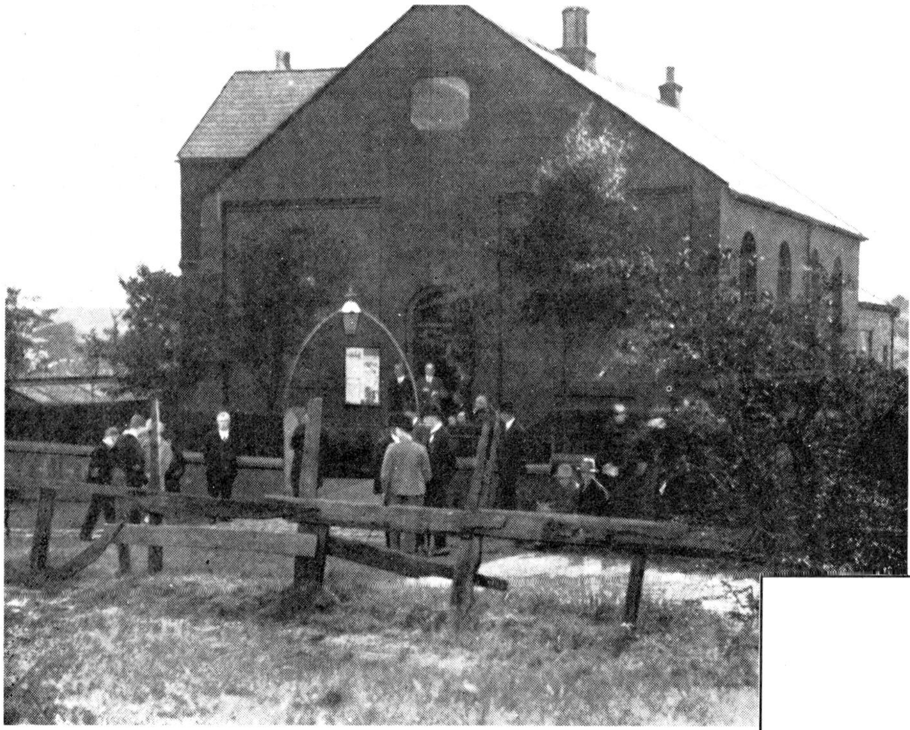

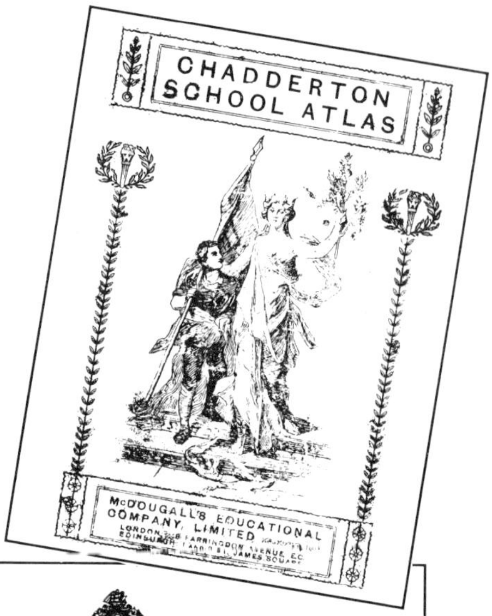

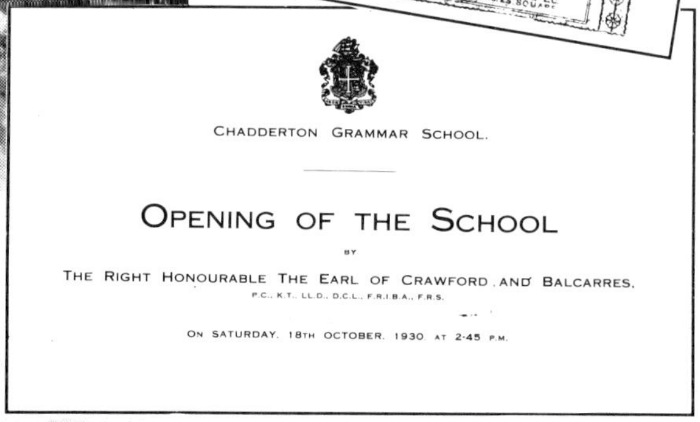

CHADDERTON GRAMMAR SCHOOL.

OPENING OF THE SCHOOL

BY

THE RIGHT HONOURABLE THE EARL OF CRAWFORD AND BALCARRES.

P.C., K.T., LL.D., D.C.L., F.R.I.B.A., F.R.S.

ON SATURDAY, 18TH OCTOBER, 1930 AT 2.45 P.M.

Above: Programme from the opening of the Grammar School which was the first co-educational grammar school built by the County Council. It became the Girls' Grammar in 1959 when a new school for boys was opened. The former is now the Radclyffe School whilst the boys' building is part of North Chadderton Comprehensive.

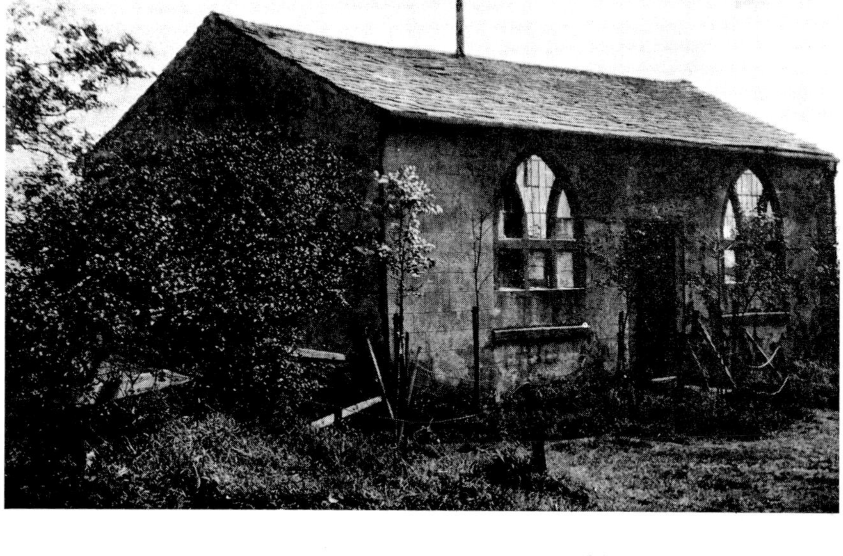

Left: The old "grammar" school at Healds Green as it appeared about seventy years ago. Built in 1789 (as the datestone above the door testifies) it is still used as a local social centre.

50 CHADDERTON EDUCATION COMMITTEE.		
LIST OF SCHOOLS IN THE DISTRICT. May, 1904.		
NAME OF SCHOOL.	Accom-mod'tion	No. on Registers
St. Matthew's Church, Mixed	} 195	87
Infants		39
St. Mark's Church, Mixed	395	214
Infants	180	94
Busk Wesleyan, Mixed	427	309
Infants	107	134
*Eustace Street Council, Mixed	620	467
Infants	260	270
St. Luke's Church, Mixed	405	338
Infants	119	138
Mills Hill Council, Mixed	180	151
Infants	130	95
Middleton Junction Coun., Mixed	282	257
Infants	110	124
Denton Lane Church, Mixed	293	202
Infants	131	111
Corpus Christi R.C., Mixed	} 598	239
Infants		92
Christ Church, Mixed	728	346
Infants	192	135
Cowhill Council, Mixed	350	294
Infants	100	126
Bourne Street Council, Mixed	382	321
Infants	142	144
Drury Lane Council, Mixed	254	262
Infants	207	219
(Stanley Road Council, Mixed)		
	6787	5208

*The accommodation at Eustace Street Mixed School is reckoned on the basis of 10 square feet per child; at all other schools 8 square feet.

Mills Hill School when it was a voluntary aided school belonging to the Baptist Church. The top photograph, taken about 1885 outside the church, shows a group of boys playing a game known by a number of names including Strong Horses, Weak Donkeys; and Dick, Trick, Talamanka, Jacko, Little Tom.

The lower photograph, dating from 1914, was taken inside the old school on Mills Hill Road. The female teacher, Miss M. Charity, was employed at the school for 34 years. From 1902 to 1944 Chadderton Council had its own Education Committee.

25

Left: The old Reform Club, Milne Street, shortly before its demolition in the early 1970's. The club dated from the 1890's and the upper storey was known as the Free Trade Hall before becoming a roller-skating rink, a dance hall and finally the Lyric Cinema.

Below: A bazaar at St. Luke's School in 1902 advertises the delights of the early cinema.

Bottom: St. Luke's Whit Walks in the 1930's. The procession turns from Broadway into Middleton Road before making its way to the joint service held in the Town Hall gardens.

HENRY BRAMLEY,	**Chadderton Botanic Stores.**	☞ For High-Class Groceries.
Mill and Property Repairer in all its Branches,	(Established over 25 years.)	**JAS. B. GUDGER,**
COMPETENT MEN IN ALL BRANCHES.	GOOD HEALTH SECURED	**Family Grocer & Tea Dealer**
Building Material on Sale.	BY USING	473, MIDDLETON ROAD,
JOINER and COFFIN-MAKER.	NATURE'S OWN REMEDIES	CHADDERTON.
Funerals completely Furnished.	APPLY:	"A POSITIVE LUXURY" 1/10 TEA.
Note the Address—	**T. DAWSON, Botanist,**	Highly Recommended.
19 GARFORTH STREET, BUSK.	393, MIDDLETON ROAD,	"A NEW RECORD" 1/4 TEA.
Workshop—DUKE STREET.	CHADDERTON.	Best Value ever offered.
POST ORDERS ATTENDED TO.		Our Speciality- STRICTLY FINEST KIEL BUTTER.
		PATENT MEDICINES, etc., etc., Lowest Cash Prices.

Above: Middleton Road about 1905, as seen from near Burnley Street. The women in traditional shawls and clogs are probably going to the local shops or even the library whose turret and dome (both features now gone) can be seen in the distance. Mr. Thomas Briggs stands at the door of number 506 whilst four doors away is the Melbourne Tavern. Modern hustle and bustle is absent with only a tramcar and horse to be seen in the roadway and a hen on the pavement in the left-hand corner! The houses were replaced in the early 1970's by the Health Centre, new Reform Club and Shopping Precinct. The Melbourne Mill was demolished in 1980 and the new retail and industrial complex now occupies the site.

The advertisements date from the first decade of this century.

The tram has reached its terminus at the Oldham boundary. To the right is Lansdowne Road, whilst the two policemen stand at the junction of Walton Street – now lost beneath the new flats. The Free Trade Inn is seen next to the ladder on the left.

27

Above: The scene in 1905 looking up Middleton Road from outside the library. Behind the high wall and trees is 'Rushbank' – three mill-owners' houses still in existence. The lower wall with railings surrounded a similar property, 'Belton Place', which became the site for the present Town Hall. The shops at the right were demolished in 1976.

Left: Middleton Road looking in the direction of the Town Hall. The photograph was taken about 1910 from opposite the Cemetery Inn (now the Harlequin). All this terrace property was cleared in the early 1970's with the exception of three public houses and Victoria Terrace (1869) near the Broadway junction.

Above: Middleton Road about 1910, looking towards the cemetery. The lamp is at the Burnley Street junction, below which can be seen the terrace row which, in the 19th century, housed the Weights and Measures Office, the first Police Station, the Office of the Local Board and the Office of the Overseer of the Poor.

Above: Middleton Road in 1962, from the boundary at Lansdowne Road. The photograph shows the mid-Victorian terrace houses and shops which were demolished by the end of the decade under the council's urban renewal programme.

Right: Nordens Road formed part of one of the oldest routes across Chadderton – from Cowhill hamlet to Chadderton Hall. This picture from about 1920 shows Springbrook House which was the focus of Chadwick's Bleach Works. In the foreground the road crosses Spring Brook by means of a foot-bridge and ford. It became a cul-de-sac during the Second World War.

The northern section of Nordens Road as it looked in the 1930's with St. Matthew's old vicarage in the distance.

29

Above: The Central Library was the gift of the American philanthropist Andrew Carnegie and was opened in 1905. The dome with flagpole above the main entrance was removed during the 1940's.

Below: Chadderton's first swimming baths. These were sanctioned by the Local Board and opened in 1894 at a cost of £6,749. The number of bathers in 1895 was almost 31,000. The baths were closed in 1935 for rebuilding.

Above: With an impressive procession and before an assembly of over 7,000 people, the War Memorial was unveiled on 8th October 1921, by Councillor Ernest Kempsey. The architects were Taylor and Simister, while Toft of London completed the figure. The photograph was probably taken at this occasion when Mr. William Whitehead laid the large wreath on behalf of the Memorial Committee.

Right: The interior of the old baths. With spectator facilities above the changing cubicles, the arrangement was the opposite to that of the new baths. The inset shows the Chadderton Water Polo Team of 1897.

Known as "Britain's greatest-ever amateur swimmer", Henry Taylor of Chadderton died in 1951 at the age of 65. During his career, which spanned half a century, he won numerous trophies including four gold Olympic medals, a record long unbroken. Three of these he gained in the London Olympics of 1908. He also held the world record for the one mile, half mile, 1500 metres, 400 metres and the Morecambe Bay Swim.

The Free Trade Hall referred to on the invitation card was above the former Reform Club on Milne Street.

URBAN DISTRICT OF CHADDERTON.

ROYAL VISIT.

Dressed as befits the occasion, the residents of 773 to 779 Middleton Road await the arrival of King George V and Queen Mary during the royal tour of Lancashire. However, little Florence Stevenson, seated at the centre, seems totally unconcerned with this historic event.

Over 3,600 children from eleven local schools were assembled at Oakbank where they sang the National Anthem to the accompaniment of the Chadderton Brass Band who were paid £5. Near them were seated 135 old age pensioners, this being 40% of the total. The council purchased 5,760 souvenir boxes of Fry's chocolate to commemorate the visit.

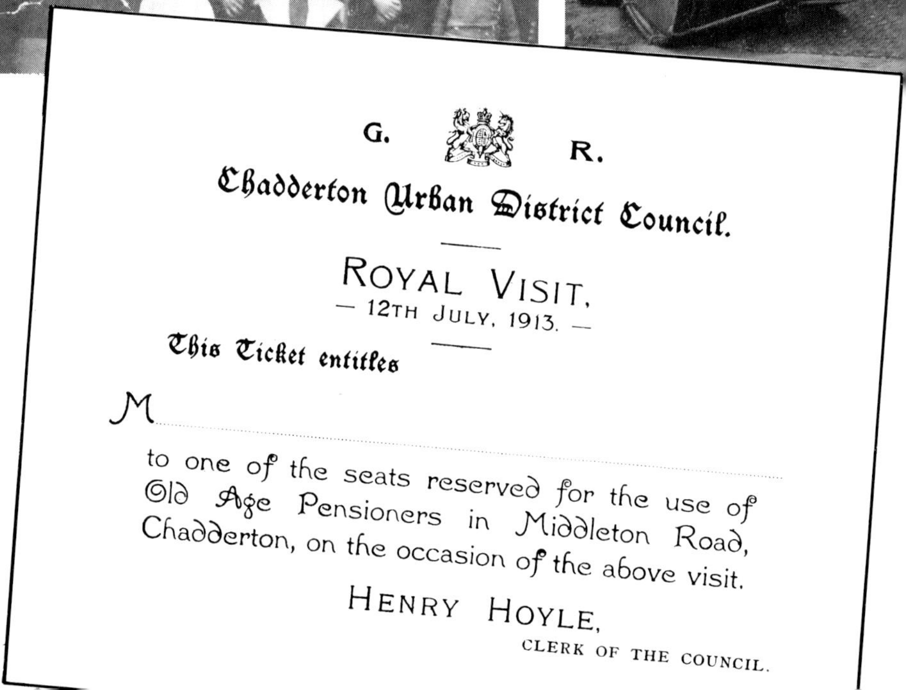

G. R.

Chadderton Urban District Council.

ROYAL VISIT.
— 12TH JULY, 1913. —

This Ticket entitles

M_____

to one of the seats reserved for the use of Old Age Pensioners in Middleton Road, Chadderton, on the occasion of the above visit.

HENRY HOYLE,
CLERK OF THE COUNCIL.

Right: The inhabitants of Whitegate Lane join in the general rejoicing at the end of the First World War. The mill in the background is the Ace, erected just before the war started.

Above: Healds Green Band in the 19th century. Founded in the 18th century the band later moved to central Chadderton where, as Chadderton Brass Band, it played the local heroes out to the Boer War and Henry Taylor home from the Olympic Games. After the Second World War members merged with the Congregational Church Band which in turn became the present Chadderton & District Band.

Right: The Town Hall illuminated and floodlit to celebrate the Silver Jubilee of King George V in May 1935.

Taken around the turn of the century, this view shows the double bridge across the Rochdale Canal near Drummer Hill. The lower swing bridge allowed the passage of barges. The trees are in the grounds of Firwood House which was owned by Mr. Lees of nearby Firwood Mill.

The boats Shamrock and Peter iced-in near Walk Mill about the turn of the century.

Left: The Duke of Bridgewater public house on the canalside near Walk Mill. Named after the pioneer of Britain's canal system, this inn provided sustenance for the bargees. Closed in 1956, it was demolished shortly afterwards.

Above: The lift bridge over the canal at Foxdenton was erected in 1928 to replace an earlier swing bridge. Unused for many years, it was dismantled in 1972.

Below: Walk Mill.

Top: Taken in 1964, this photograph shows the dismantling of the Werneth Incline on the Middleton Junction to Oldham line which opened in 1842. With a gradient of 1 in 27 this section of railway was the steepest passenger line in Britain. The house was Railway View, and this was demolished shortly afterwards.

Above: Middleton Junction station on the line from Manchester to Leeds was opened in 1842 when the branch line to Oldham was constructed. It closed in 1966. The bridge is the original one of 1839.
The inset picture (right) shows the station shortly before closure with the line to Rochdale on the left and the branch line to Oldham and the Chadderton Goods Yard to the right.

This railway bridge at Mills Hill, dating from 1839, was replaced by the present one in 1934. The new one allowed double deck trams and, in 1935, buses to operate through Chadderton.

The tramway along Middleton Road opened in 1902 and was operated by the privately owned Middleton Electric Traction Company whose service finished at the boundary with Oldham. In 1925 the local section was purchased by Chadderton Council who handed it over to Oldham Corporation to operate. The final tram ran in 1935. The top picture, taken about 1924, shows a M.E.T.Co. tramcar passing the Hunt Lane Tavern, whilst the lower picture from 1930 is of an Oldham car at the junction with Broadway. The shop, which was next to the cemetery, was demolished about 1960.

Chadderton Arms
BROADWAY　　　　CHADDERTON

Modern, up-to-date, and carefully planned for the convenience and comfort of the public.

Luxurious Lounge, Smoke Rooms, Dining Room, etc., Central Heating.

Excellent facilities for Wedding Parties and similar functions in the spacious Clubroom, an ideal place to entertain your friends.

Good parking space.

Bowling Green and Gardens will be completed at an early date.

DECIDEDLY A HOUSE YOU MUST VISIT

....

WILSON'S ALES AND STOUT
in perfect condition.

WEMBLEY BOTTLED BEERS
also

Bass, Guinness and Worthington in bottle　　Spirits, Wines Liqueurs, etc.

....

JOHN T. WHITE　-　-　Proprietor

Top left and right: Steam excavators constructing the canal bridge section next to the Boat and Horses public house in 1925.

Below: Happy days indeed as this charabanc sets out from the Nimble Nook Working Mens Club, Foxdenton Lane, sometime in the twenties.

Above: Driving on the wrong side of Broadway didn't seem to pose problems back in the 1930's! This leisurely scene was captured just below Hunt Lane at Spring Bank.

"The construction of this great arterial road . . . would confer untold benefits on Chadderton in the days to come". These words by Councillor James Fitton, Chairman of the Urban District Council in February 1922, were certainly prophetic for the construction of Broadway welded together the many hamlets of the township and prepared the way for all subsequent modern development.

Above: The scene in April 1907 at Cowhill when a runaway train belonging to Platts textile engineers overran the sidings and plunged into Walsh Street. The building is the Crown Inn, known then and now as the "sump 'ole" – a connection with the former coal mines of the locality.

Right: This accident took place in December 1909, on Thompson Lane near Fields New Road. The driver was unhurt as his "motor lurry" was partially buried when the road subsided.

This small square at Coalshaw Green stood opposite Turf Lane. The scene taken about 1915 shows the aftermath of one of the floods common in that area.

Glebe Street at Coalshaw Green also under flood. Notice the 'Sign of the Clog' outside the local footwear shop!

On 11th July 1927, in the early evening, a cloudburst caused the River Irk to overflow its banks with devastating results. The boating lake in Chadderton Hall Park was also washed away, whilst near Mills Hill the aqueduct carrying the Rochdale Canal over the river was breached. The culvert which carried the river under the railway embankment was blocked by debris causing a large lake to form. The council set up a relief fund and collection boxes were in evidence for the many spectators who came to see the damage.

Below: The water from the burst canal aqueduct cascaded into the River Irk increasing its volume still further. The chimney in the background belonged to McDougall's chemical works.

Above: The bridge next to the Church Inn was the only local one to survive as the swollen River Irk swept through Chadderton Fold.

Bottom: Cragclough cottages near the Fold soon became victims of the uncontrollable waters.

Although dependent on a plant native to distant lands and springing up in a remote and sparsely populated county, the Lancashire cotton industry contributed greatly to the supremacy of Britain during the nineteenth century. It reached its peak shortly before the First World War and since then has been in decline.

At the beginning of this century 6,000 people, a quarter of its population, worked in Chadderton's mills. In the mid-1920's over four and a half million spindles still spun cotton in over 50 mills. Today the industry survives in only three mills – the Chadderton, Elk and Kent and the landscape has been largely cleared of these industrial giants.

Below: In 1920, at the age of 13, Harry Pleasant left Denton Lane School to start work as a little piecer at the Glenby Mill on Lansdowne Road. It was his job to rejoin any threads which broke during the spinning process. His father, Walter, a mule spinner, stands behind whilst the female operative is their creeler. She was responsible for restocking the frame in the background with bobbins of the loose roving which was then stretched and twisted into the thread. There would also be doffers who took off the cops or tubes of thread once they were full.

Above: The Magnet Mill, Denton Lane, was opened in 1902, and demolished in 1966. The 1700 h.p. engine was by George Saxon of Manchester. The flywheel in the background carried the ropes which drove the machinery on the different floors.

Below: Artist's impression of the Sun Mill, built in the 1860's, and one of the largest in the county. It was founded as a Workers' Co-operative and was also the first textile limited liability company in Lancashire. In 1867 it was visited by William Ewart Gladstone who was to become Prime Minister in the following year. It was demolished in 1986.

Although coal mining in Chadderton is mentioned in the fourteenth century, it wasn't until the seventeenth that it was mined to any extent. By the end of the nineteenth century shafts had been sunk at Buckley Wood, Birchen Bower, Cowhill, Hunt Clough and Ferny Field.

Stockfield Colliery, Cowhill, in 1910. The miners prepare for the afternoon shift and each carries his safety lamp. The man at the right was the deputy or fireman and beside him can be seen a canister of explosives. The mill in the background is the Palm, which was demolished in 1926.

Birchen Bower Colliery in the early years of this century. When it closed in the 1920's it was Chadderton's last coal mine.

The contribution of the Chadderton factory of British Aerospace to the defence of the nation, both in peacetime and wartime, is a significant one. During the war years it turned out 3,050 Avro Lancasters – the greatest bomber of World War Two. This represented more than 40% of the total built.

 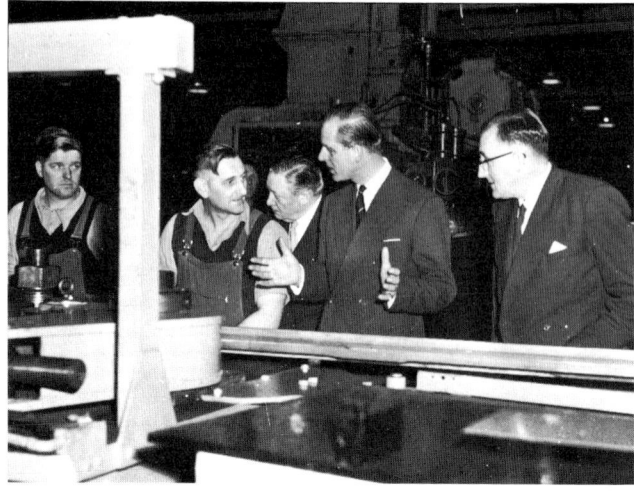

Above left: Lancaster production in 1944.

Above right: The visit of H.R.H. Prince Philip on 8th November 1955.

Left: Exterior view of the A. V. Roe factory, Greengate, in the 1940's.

Below: The mighty Vulcan, the world's first four-jet, delta-wing bomber. It was used during the Falklands conflict in 1982, over 30 years after it first came off the assembly line.

Above: The result of one of the few bombs that fell on Chadderton during World War Two is seen in this picture of Foxdenton Lane.

During the war the people of Chadderton adopted the warship 'Circe' (a plaque commemorating this may be seen on the Town Hall balcony). When the war ended the sailors showed their gratitude by bringing back a supply of bananas for the children of the local schools who had never seen this fruit.

In the picture (above), taken in May 1946 outside Mills Hill School, is the Chairman of the Council, Councillor Edwin Buckley, with on the far right, Mr. G. Tiffin, Chief Education Officer for Lancashire Division 23 which was based in Chadderton.

Above: Two aerial views from 1933 taken by N. S. Roberts. Broadway cuts across the top right-hand corner whilst the rows of terrace houses mark out Middleton Road. To the left of the extensive cemetery, which was opened in 1857, can be seen the industrial hamlet of Chadwick's Bleach and Print Works. This was demolished in the mid-1980's. The railway sidings to Chadderton Goods Yard run across the bottom right of the picture.

Above: In this view of south Chadderton the railway line from Failsworth to Oldham crosses from left to top right with the bridge over Stanley Road clearly visible. Below centre can be seen Corpus Christi Catholic Church, which was then newly opened. The large number of mills along Fields New Road is very apparent in the top left of the picture.